HOUGHTON MIFFLIN HARCOURT

Write-In Reader

Grade 1 Vol. 2

Copyright © by Houghton Mifflin Harcourt Publishing Company

All rights reserved. No part of this work may be reproduced or transmitted in any form or by any means, electronic or mechanical, including photocopying or recording, or by any information storage and retrieval system, without the prior written permission of the copyright owner unless such copying is expressly permitted by federal copyright law. Requests for permission to make copies of any part of the work should be addressed to Houghton Mifflin Harcourt Publishing Company, Attn: Contracts, Copyrights, and Licensing, 9400 South Park Center Loop, Orlando, Florida 32819.

Printed in the U.S.A.

ISBN 978-0-547-87419-7

14 15 16 17 18 19 20   0877   21 20 19 18 17 16 15

4500521497   A B C D E F G

If you have received these materials as examination copies free of charge, Houghton Mifflin Harcourt Publishing Company retains title to the materials and they may not be resold. Resale of examination copies is strictly prohibited.

Possession of this publication in print format does not entitle users to convert this publication, or any portion of it, into electronic format.

 HOUGHTON MIFFLIN HARCOURT
School Publishers

Contents

✓ WORDS TO KNOW

around

because

before

light

Outer Space

Complete the sentence.
Check the best word.

1 It lets off smoke _____ it is hot.

☐ because   ☐ around

2 He set up his flag _____ he left.

☐ light   ☐ before

3 Green rings spin _____ it.

☐ around ☐ before

4 This man felt as _____ as dust.

☐ because ☐ light

Copyright © by Houghton Mifflin Harcourt Publishing Company. All rights reserved.

Write a Word

Read the words in the word box.
Write the word under the picture.

hose	note
robe	rose

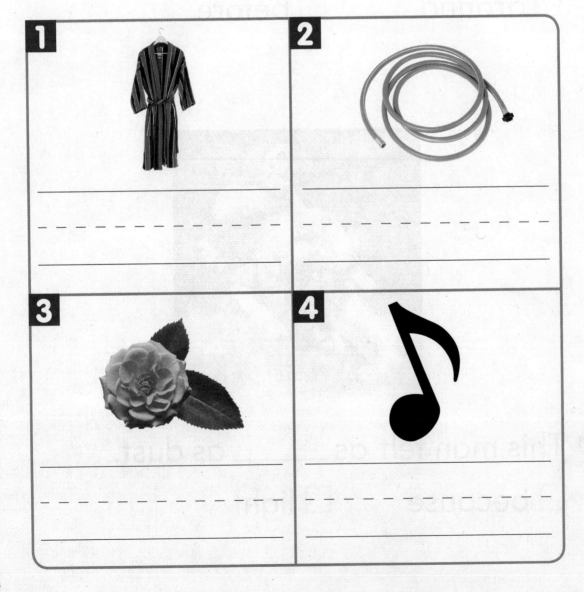

1

_____

- - - - - - - - - - -

_____

2

_____

- - - - - - - - - - -

_____

3

_____

- - - - - - - - - - -

_____

4

_____

- - - - - - - - - - -

_____

Bo's Big Space Trip

by Megan Linke

Copyright © by Houghton Mifflin Harcourt Publishing Company. All rights reserved.

Bo sat in his space ship.

He set its knobs and switches.

"Space trip!" yelled Bo. "Go, go, go!"

But his mom said, "Lunch time!"

Little Bo had big plans.

He had his map.

"Space trip!" yelled Bo. "Go, go, go!"

But his mom said, "Bed time!"

"Rest, Bo," said Mom.
"Rest **before** you go."
"OK," said Bo. "If I must."

Copyright © by Houghton Mifflin Harcourt Publishing Company. All rights reserved.

Then Bo rose up, up, up!

His ship puffed smoke.

Bo felt as **light** as dust!

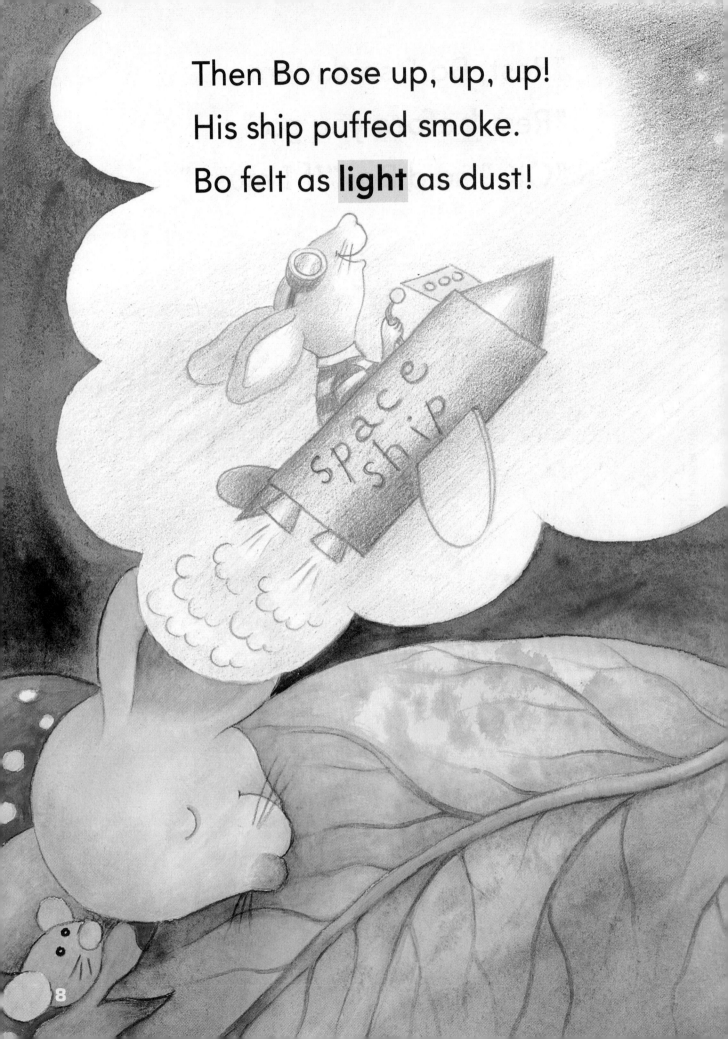

8

Huge dots shone all **around** him.

Bo felt little **because** space was so big.

Little Bo missed his mom.

Copyright © by Houghton Mifflin Harcourt Publishing Company. All rights reserved.

Then Bo woke up.

He gave his mom a hug.

"Space is fun," said Bo.

"But I am glad to be home."

Look Back and Respond

Read Together

Check the answer.

1 What is the main idea of this story?

☐ Little Bo wants to go to space.

☐ Little Bo has a map.

2 What does Bo's space ship have?

☐ stars   ☐ switches

3 Check a detail from Bo's trip.

☐ Bo has glasses on.

☐ Bo's mom comes with him.

Write about Bo's trip.

4 Did Bo really go to space?

_____

_ _

_____

Copyright © by Houghton Mifflin Harcourt Publishing Company. All rights reserved.

11

Return to

"Let's Go to the Moon!"
by Stephen R. Swinburne

"Let's Go to the Moon!"
Student Book pp. 15–35

Be a Reading Detective!

Look back at "Let's Go to the Moon!"
Think about the questions.
Look for clues.

1 **What** can you see on the moon?

2 **How** do people get to the moon?

Write or draw your answer.

1 **What** can you see on the moon?

Talk about question 2.

Tell about the clues you found.

2 **How** do people get to the moon?

Copyright © by Houghton Mifflin Harcourt Publishing Company. All rights reserved.

✓ **WORDS TO KNOW**

by

car

don't

sure

Let's Go on a Trip

Complete the sentence.

Check the best word.

1 We can go _by_ bus.

☑ by ☐ car

2 That bike slips, so _____ take it.

☐ don't ☐ by

Copyright © by Houghton Mifflin Harcourt Publishing Company. All rights reserved.

3 Let's go in Dad's _____.

☐ sure ☐ car

4 I am _____ we will not be late!

☐ don't ☐ sure

Read the words in the word box.
Write the word under the picture.

beak	bee
seat	feet

Pops

Rex

Lee

Ace

Pink

Pops Takes a Trip

by Marc Vargas

Copyright © by Houghton Mifflin Harcourt Publishing Company. All rights reserved.

Pops sat in his **car**.

"Here I go!" he said.

"Can I go?" asked Rex.

15

"OK," said Pops.

"Be **sure** you **don't** sit on Lee."

Lee did not speak.

He just said, "Squeak."

Copyright © by Houghton Mifflin Harcourt Publishing Company. All rights reserved.

"Me, me!" yelled Ace.

"This will be fun!"

So Ace got in back.

Clunk! Bang! Clank!

Pink got in as well.

"No seat for me?" asked Pops.

"Must I go **by** bike?"

Copyright © by Houghton Mifflin Harcourt Publishing Company. All rights reserved.

"Yup!" said Rex.

Then Pink made space.

"Sit by me, Pops!" she said.

"Thanks, Pink," said Pops.

And off they went.

Beep! Beep! Beep!

Check the answer.

1 Who has the car?

☐ Ace ☐ Pops

2 What sounds does Ace make in the car?

☐ clunk, bang, clank

☐ beep, beep, beep

3 Who makes space for Pops?

☐ Rex ☐ Pink

Write about a place you went.

_____

4 I went to _____ .

Copyright © by Houghton Mifflin Harcourt Publishing Company. All rights reserved.

Return to

Be a Reading Detective!

Look back at "The Big Trip." Think about the questions. Look for clues.

"The Big Trip"
Student Book pp. 53–73

1 **Who** are the characters?

2 **What** happens at the end of the story?

Write or draw your answer.

1 **Who** are the characters?

Talk about question 2.

Tell about the clues you found.

2 **What** happens at the end of the story?

Copyright © by Houghton Mifflin Harcourt Publishing Company. All rights reserved.

✓ **WORDS TO KNOW**

first

sometimes

these

under

Let's Eat!

Complete the sentence.
Check the best word.

1 Eat lots of _____ grains.

☐ first ☐ these

2 Kay eats sweets _____.

☐ sometimes ☐ under

3 Gail's place mat is _____ her plate.

☐ these ☐ under

4 Ray drinks his milk ___ at each meal.

☐ these ☐ first

Copyright © by Houghton Mifflin Harcourt Publishing Company. All rights reserved.

Read the words in the word box.
Write the word under the picture.

pail	pay
snail	rain

1

_____
- - - - - - - - - - -
_____

2

_____
- - - - - - - - - - -
_____

3

_____
- - - - - - - - - - -
_____

4

_____
- - - - - - - - - - -
_____

Ant's Grand Feast

by Megan Linke

Copyright © by Houghton Mifflin Harcourt Publishing Company. All rights reserved.

Seats got kicked back.

And kids left to play.

But they did not clean up.

This is my day!

An ant can eat lots.

So **first** let me say,

I can eat, eat, eat, eat,

Each week and each day.

Copyright © by Houghton Mifflin Harcourt Publishing Company. All rights reserved.

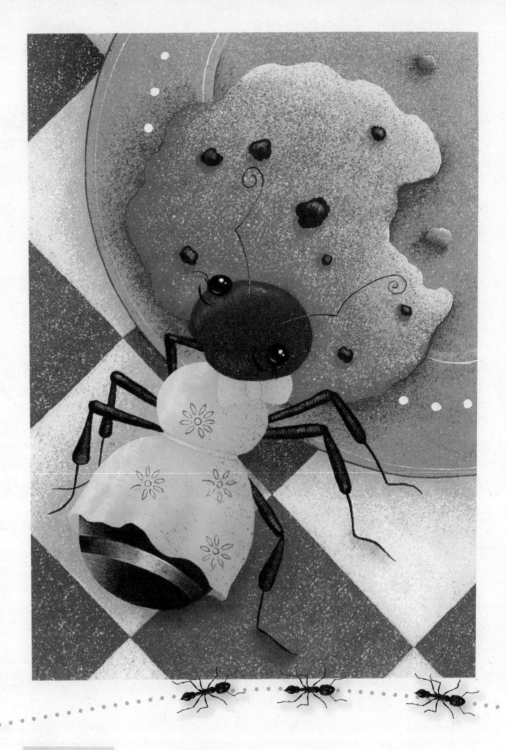

These crumbs may be trash,

But as we can see,

Sometimes trash is a feast,

For an ant such as me!

See this? It's still fresh!

It sat **under** that plate.

It's as big as I am,

But I will eat it. Just wait!

Copyright © by Houghton Mifflin Harcourt Publishing Company. All rights reserved.

Well, well! I am stuffed!
I am too stuffed to think,
But I wish that I had
Just a little to drink.

But I ate so much,
And I am in such pain!
So I think I will stay here
And wait till it rains.

Check the answer.

1 Why was this story written?

☐ for fun

☐ to teach us what to eat

2 How was this story told?

☐ only in pictures

☐ in rhymes and pictures

3 In the end, why does Ant rest?

☐ She is full.   ☐ She is scared.

Write about your favorite food.

4 I like to eat _____.

Copyright © by Houghton Mifflin Harcourt Publishing Company. All rights reserved.

Return to

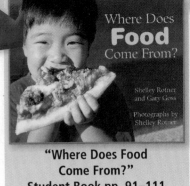

"Where Does Food Come From?" Student Book pp. 91–111

Be a Reading Detective!

Look back at "Where Does Food Come From?"

Think about the questions.

Look for clues.

1 **What** do people eat?

2 **How** are different foods made?

Write or draw your answer.

1 **What** do people eat?

Talk about question 2.
Tell about the clues you found.

2 **How** are different foods made?

Copyright © by Houghton Mifflin Harcourt Publishing Company. All rights reserved.

✓ **WORDS TO KNOW**

great

paper

soon

work

When We Grow Up

Complete the sentence.

Check the best word.

1 Sam will make a ＿＿＿ vet.

☐ paper ☐ great

2 Joan will ＿＿＿ at home like Dad.

☐ work ☐ soon

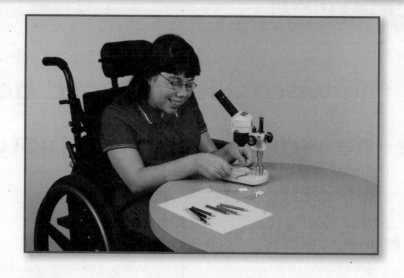

3 Jane will take notes on _____.

☐ great   ☐ paper

4 We will grow up _____!

☐ soon   ☐ work

Copyright © by Houghton Mifflin Harcourt Publishing Company. All rights reserved.

Write a Word

Read the words in the word box.

Write the word under the picture.

soap	crow
boat	snow

1

2

3

4

When Tom Grows Up

by Diane Bird

Copyright © by Houghton Mifflin Harcourt Publishing Company. All rights reserved.

Tom sat on his mom's knee.

"When I grow up," said Tom,

"I will write like this. I will paint, too!"

Each day, Tom did his spelling drills.

But he did not moan and groan.

He could not wait to write.

Copyright © by Houghton Mifflin Harcourt Publishing Company. All rights reserved.

Then Tom got a paint set as a gift.

Tom glowed. "This is **great**!" he said.

He picked up some **paper**.

Tom painted and painted.

He showed his paintings to his pals.

"This is not bad," his pals said.

Tom had set his goal.

He had to **work** at it.

But he did not quit.

Copyright © by Houghton Mifflin Harcourt Publishing Company. All rights reserved.

Tom's work **soon** paid off.

These days, Tom writes for kids.

And he paints for them, too!

Copyright © by Houghton Mifflin Harcourt Publishing Company. All rights reserved.

Look Back and Respond — Read Together

Check the answer.

1 **What does Tom want to do?**

☐ teach kids ☐ write stories

2 **When does Tom make up his mind?**

☐ as a kid ☐ as a grownup

3 **Which happens first?**

☐ Tom gets a paint set.

☐ Tom reads with his mom.

Write about yourself.

4 **What will you be when you grow up?**

_____

- -

_____

Return to

Be a Reading Detective!

Look back at "Tomás Rivera."
Think about the questions.
Look for clues.

"Tomás Rivera"
Student Book pp. 129–143

1 **What** did Tomás Rivera do?

2 **Who** helped Tomás?

Write or draw your answer.

1 **What** did Tomás Rivera do?

Talk about question 2.
Tell about the clues you found.

2 **Who** helped Tomás?

Copyright © by Houghton Mifflin Harcourt Publishing Company. All rights reserved.

Nature

more

old

try

want

Complete the sentence.

Check the best word.

1 This tree is very _____.

☐ old ☐ more

2 The foxes will _____ to find food.

☐ want ☐ try

3 It will pick up _____ pinecones.

☐ more ☐ try

4 We _____ to keep this place clean!

☐ old ☐ want

Copyright © by Houghton Mifflin Harcourt Publishing Company. All rights reserved.

Read the words in the word box.
Write the word under the picture.

peanut	mailbox
seashell	sailboat

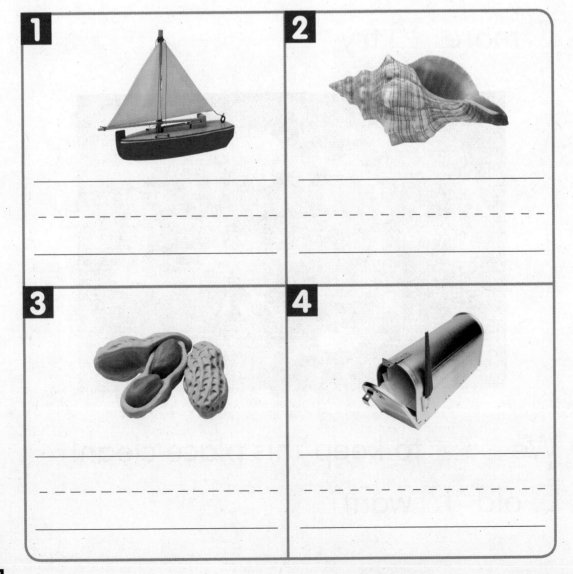

44

Tree Frog Sings His Song

by Megan Linke

In the **old** days, Tree Frog was glad.

He sang and sang, all day long.

"Jip-jip, croak!" he sang. "Jip-jip, croak!"

Copyright © by Houghton Mifflin Harcourt Publishing Company. All rights reserved.

Tree Frog did not have many fans.

"He thinks he can sing!" said Duck.

"What a joke," buzzed Bug.

Copyright © by Houghton Mifflin Harcourt Publishing Company. All rights reserved.

At last, Duck made him stop.

"Quit singing!" Duck said.

"No one likes that song."

Tree Frog was crushed.

Tree Frog hid himself in his tree.

Then a face came and peeked at him.

"Hush," she said. "**Try** and cheer up."

Copyright © by Houghton Mifflin Harcourt Publishing Company. All rights reserved.

"I cannot," Tree Frog sniffed.

"No one likes my song."

"I like it!" said his new pal.

"I **want** you to sing **more**."

At that, Tree Frog leapt up.

These days, Tree Frog sings at sunset.

And he is as glad as can be.

Look Back and Respond

Read Together

Check the answer.

1 Why did Duck talk to Tree Frog?

☐ to tell him to quit singing

☐ to tell him he should sing

2 How did Duck make Tree Frog feel?

☐ very sad

☐ angry

3 What made Tree Frog happy?

☐ The moon liked his song.

☐ Duck said, "I'm sorry."

Write about Tree Frog's new pal.

_____

4 She is _____ .

Copyright © by Houghton Mifflin Harcourt Publishing Company. All rights reserved.

Return to

"Little Rabbit's Tale"
Student Book pp. 161–179

Be a Reading Detective!

Look back at "Little Rabbit's Tale."

Think about the questions.

Look for clues.

1 **Who** are the characters?

2 **What** scares Little Rabbit?

Write or draw your answer.

1 **Who** are the characters?

Copyright © by Houghton Mifflin Harcourt Publishing Company. All rights reserved.

Talk about question 2.
Tell about the clues you found.

2 **What** scares Little Rabbit?

Grow, Garden, Grow!

Complete the sentence.

Check the best word.

1 Plants grow day and _____.

☐ night   ☐ noise

2 Bugs in the yard make _____.

☐ noise   ☐ world

Copyright © by Houghton Mifflin Harcourt Publishing Company. All rights reserved.

3 In springtime, the ____ is green!

☐ world   ☐ few

4 We just need a ____ more seeds.

☐ few   ☐ night

53

Read the words in the word box.
Write the word under the picture.

star	jar
yarn	shark

1 _____

2 _____

3 _____

4 _____

Bean Reaches for the Sun

by Megan Linke

Copyright © by Houghton Mifflin Harcourt Publishing Company. All rights reserved.

Bean woke up late at **night**.

He felt sore after resting in his hard bed.

He did not see a thing.

He did not hear a **noise**.

His **world** was cold and dark.

Then he felt a spark.

He started to stretch and take form.

He inched up.

He rose up more and more.

Copyright © by Houghton Mifflin Harcourt Publishing Company. All rights reserved.

Then the ground parted!

Bean reached up his bent arm.

He reached up, up, up for the sun!

At the same time, he shot down.
He stretched, twisted, and held fast.
He felt strong and safe and at home.

Copyright © by Houghton Mifflin Harcourt Publishing Company. All rights reserved

A wide, blue space stretched over him.

Gusts of wind lifted him up.

A **few** ants went marching by.

The sun felt so nice.

Bean held his head up.

He felt like yelling, "Here I am, World!"

He felt glad to be a plant.

Look Back and Respond

Check the answer.

1 Who is the main character?

☐ Bean, a plant ☐ Bean, a boy

2 Where is Bean growing?

☐ in a pot, inside

☐ in the ground, outside

3 Why does Bean feel a spark?

☐ He is growing.

☐ He is waking up.

Write about how Bean feels at the end.

4 He feels _____

Copyright © by Houghton Mifflin Harcourt Publishing Company. All rights reserved.

Return to

"The Garden"
Student Book pp. 15–29

Be a Reading Detective!

Look back at "The Garden." Think about the questions. Look for clues.

1 **Where** does the story happen?

2 **What** is Toad trying to do?

Write or draw your answer.

1 **Where** does the story happen?

Talk about question 2.

Tell about the clues you found.

2 **What** is Toad trying to do?

Copyright © by Houghton Mifflin Harcourt Publishing Company. All rights reserved.

✓ **WORDS TO KNOW**

baby
follow
learning
until

Birds of a Feather

Complete the sentence.

Check the best word.

1 This crane glides _____ it needs rest.

☐ until   ☐ follow

2 The little ducks _____ their mom.

☐ until   ☐ follow

Copyright © by Houghton Mifflin Harcourt Publishing Company. All rights reserved.

3 A mother bird feeds her ____.

☐ baby ☐ learning

4 This chick is ____ to feed itself.

☐ baby ☐ learning

Read the words in the word box.

Write the word under the picture.

bird   dirt

fern   nurse

1

2

3

4

Copyright © by Houghton Mifflin Harcourt Publishing Company. All rights reserved.

Peacock and Crane

by Megan Linke

One day, Peacock met Crane.

"I feel bad for you," chirped Peacock.

"Being dull and gray is such a bore."

It was not a nice thing for him to say.

But Crane did not feel hurt.

"I am fine being this way," said Crane.

"Is that so?" asked Peacock.

Copyright © by Houghton Mifflin Harcourt Publishing Company. All rights reserved.

"Yes, it is!" said Crane. "See this?
Cranes can glide for miles and miles."
Crane spread his long wings.
He whirled and turned in the wind.

It seemed like such fun!

Peacock wished he could **follow** Crane.

He beat his wings **until** he lifted off.

But he did not glide like Crane did.

Copyright © by Houghton Mifflin Harcourt Publishing Company. All rights reserved.

"I first did this as a **baby**," said Crane.

"**Learning** it was not hard.

You are quite pretty, Peacock.

But you will never glide like me."

Peacock sat thinking.

For the first time in his life, he got it.

All birds were gifted, not just him!

Each bird was great in its own way.

Look Back and Respond

Read Together

Check the answer.

1 Which word best describes Peacock?

☐ proud ☐ funny

2 What can Crane do?

☐ glide ☐ puff up

3 What lesson does Peacock learn?

☐ how to fly for miles

☐ that all birds are special

Write about yourself.

4 What makes you special?

_____

- - - - - - - - - - - - - - - - - -

_____

Copyright © by Houghton Mifflin Harcourt Publishing Company. All rights reserved.

Return to

"Amazing Animals"
Student Book pp. 47–65

Be a Reading Detective!

Look back at "Amazing
Animals."
Think about the questions.
Look for clues.

1 **What** is the selection about?

2 **How** is a turtle's shell helpful?

Write or draw your answer.

1 **What** is the selection about?

Copyright © by Houghton Mifflin Harcourt Publishing Company. All rights reserved.

Talk about question 2.
Tell about the clues you found.

2 **How** is a turtle's shell helpful?

again

began

nothing

together

Pet Pals

Complete the sentence.

Check the best word.

1 Their dog Chip ___ to run.

☐ began   ☐ together

2 Brook and her cat sat ___.

☐ nothing   ☐ together

3 Max has ___ in his bowl.
  ☐ nothing ☐ again

4 Shane fed her fish ___.
  ☐ began ☐ again

Copyright © by Houghton Mifflin Harcourt Publishing Company. All rights reserved.

Read the words in the word box.
Write the word under the picture.

woods	book
cook	hook

1

_____

- - - - - - - - - -

_____

2

_____

- - - - - - - - - -

_____

3

_____

- - - - - - - - - -

_____

4

_____

- - - - - - - - - -

_____

Rex   Pup   Muff   Kids at Home

Pet Dreams
by Paolo Rizzi

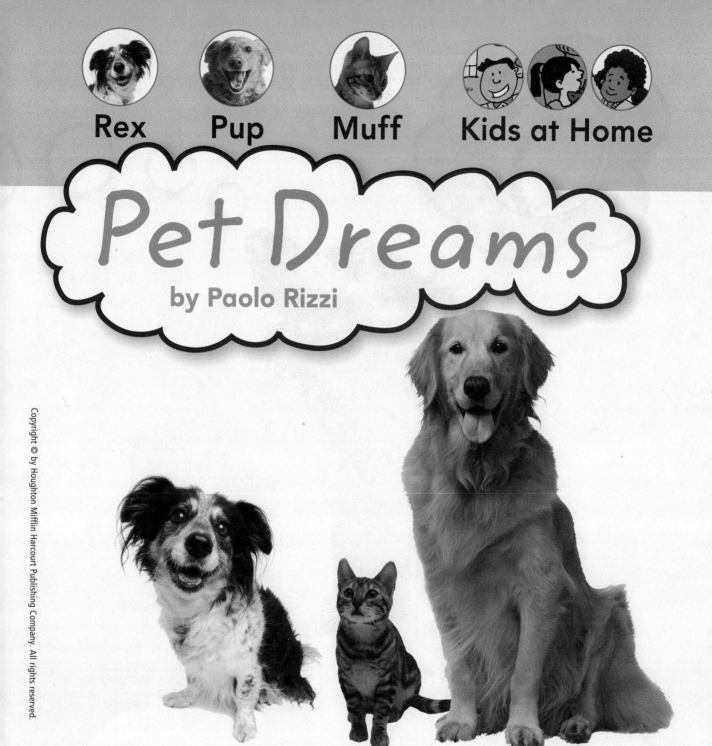

Rex, Muff, and Pup sat dreaming **together**.

"Being a pet is such a bore," Muff said.

"My kid at home is just no fun."

Muff shook her head.

Copyright © by Houghton Mifflin Harcourt Publishing Company. All rights reserved.

"I know," said Rex.
"My kid at home just plays catch.
Back and forth, time and **again**!"

"If he'd just chase things with me,"
Rex said, "that would be good!"

Copyright © by Houghton Mifflin Harcourt Publishing Company. All rights reserved.

"Yes, **nothing** beats hunting," said Muff.
"My kid just tosses fake mice.
That is no fun.
I wish she'd go bird hunting with me!"

Copyright © by Houghton Mifflin Harcourt Publishing Company. All rights reserved.

"What I hate," said Pup, "is bath time.
If I could just take mud baths!
That would be good."

Just then, dinner bells **began** ringing.

At that, Muff stood up.

"Woof, woof!" yelled Rex and Pup.

And the pets all ran off home.

Read Together

Check the answer.

1 Why is Rex mad at his owner?

☐ His owner just plays catch.

☐ His owner chases chipmunks.

2 What does Pup want in his bath?

☐ mud ☐ soap

3 What makes the pets go home?

☐ dinner bells ringing

☐ their owners calling

Write about the pets' dreams.

_____

4 - - - - - - - - - - - - - - - - - -

_____

Copyright © by Houghton Mifflin Harcourt Publishing Company. All rights reserved.

Return to

"Whistle for Willie"
Student Book pp. 83–103

Be a Reading Detective!

Look back at "Whistle for Willie."

Think about the questions.

Look for clues.

1 Where does Willie play?

2 How does Willie learn to whistle?

Write or draw your answer.

1 **Where** does Willie play?

(empty answer box)

Talk about question 2.
Tell about the clues you found.

2 **How** does Willie learn to whistle?

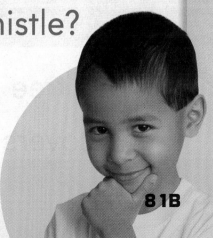

Copyright © by Houghton Mifflin Harcourt Publishing Company. All rights reserved.

almost

covers

ready

soil

These Trees

Complete the sentence. Check the best word.

1 Seeds grow in _____.

☐ covers   ☐ soil

2 This tree _____ the yard with leaves.

☐ covers   ☐ ready

3 He is _____ to plant his tree.

☐ almost

☐ ready

4 I am _____ as big as this tree!

☐ soil ☐ almost

Copyright © by Houghton Mifflin Harcourt Publishing Company. All rights reserved.

Read the words in the word box.
Write the word under the picture.

moon	spoon
boot	screw

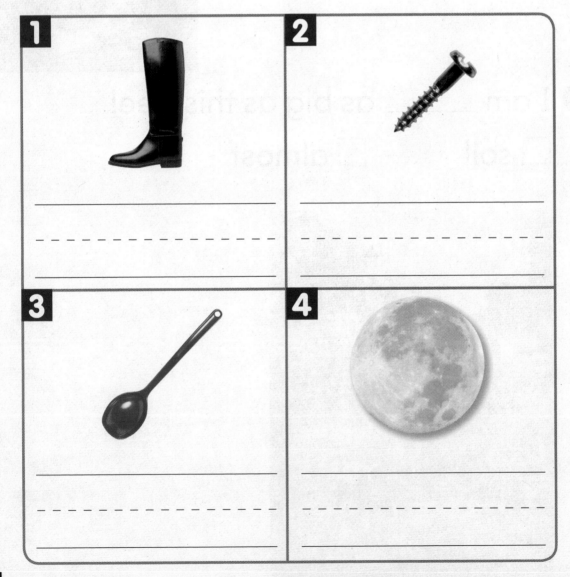

1

_____

- - - - - - - - - -

2

_____

- - - - - - - - - -

3

_____

- - - - - - - - - -

4

_____

- - - - - - - - - -

How to Plant a Tree

by Paolo Rizzi

Copyright © by Houghton Mifflin Harcourt Publishing Company. All rights reserved.

1 ▷ Get set.

Pick a good spot to plant your tree.

It will need space to grow.

Find tools you will need.

You are **almost ready**!

85

2 ▶ Dig it.

Look at your tree's roots.

Dig a hole that its roots will fit in.

The hole must be twice as wide.

Use tools that will help you dig.

Copyright © by Houghton Mifflin Harcourt Publishing Company. All rights reserved.

3 ▶ **Plant it.**

Check that the tree's roots are loose.

They cannot be too packed.

Then, place the tree in the hole.

4 ▷ Fill it in.

Fill in the hole.

Make sure the **soil** **covers** the roots.

Scoop it in, and then pack it down.

Copyright © by Houghton Mifflin Harcourt Publishing Company. All rights reserved.

5 Keep it wet.

Next, soak your tree with water.

Check on your new tree for a few weeks.

Check that its soil stays damp.

6 Let it grow!

It will take time, but that little tree will grow.

Soon, you will see your work pay off!

Check the answer.

1 Which step comes first?

☐ Find a spot.

☐ Check the roots.

2 What happens last?

☐ The tree grows.

☐ The tree is watered.

3 Why should you check on a new tree?

☐ so the soil stays damp

☐ so the roots stay packed

4 Write one step in planting a tree.

_____

- - - - - - - - - - - - - - - - - - -

_____

Copyright © by Houghton Mifflin Harcourt Publishing Company. All rights reserved.

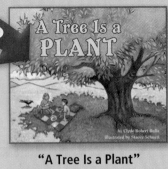

Return to

"A Tree Is a Plant"
Student Book pp. 121–147

Be a Reading Detective!

Look back at "A Tree Is a
Plant."

Think about the questions.
Look for clues.

1 **What** is a seed?

2 **How** does an apple tree change?

91A

Write or draw your answer.

1 **What** is a seed?

Talk about question 2.
Tell about the clues you found.

2 **How** does an apple tree change?

Copyright © by Houghton Mifflin Harcourt Publishing Company. All rights reserved.

buy
family
myself
please

Moving Day

Complete the sentence.
Check the best word.

1 A new _____ will live next door.

☐ family ☐ buy

2 I will _____ them a gift.

☐ family ☐ buy

3 Can you ____ help lift this box?

☐ myself ☐ please

Sarah's Room

4 I cannot pick it up by ____.

☐ myself ☐ please

Copyright © by Houghton Mifflin Harcourt Publishing Company. All rights reserved.

Read the words in the word box.
Write the word under the picture.

cow   owl

couch   cloud

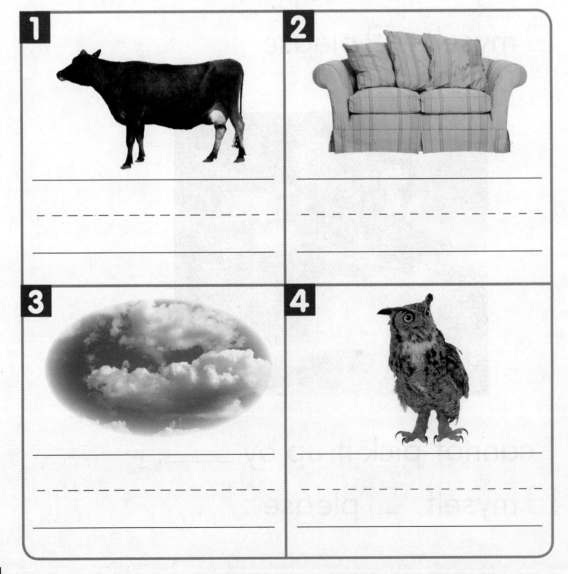

1

2

3

4

Who Will It Be?

by Marvin Hampton

Copyright © by Houghton Mifflin Harcourt Publishing Company. All rights reserved.

Raccoon went out to sweep his step.

As he swept, a big truck drove up.

"Did an animal **buy** that house?" he asked.

"Who will it be?"

"I hope it's not a crab," thought Raccoon.
"Crabs are quite proud and not too nice.
Crabs can pinch, too!"

Copyright © by Houghton Mifflin Harcourt Publishing Company. All rights reserved.

"Maybe it will be an ox.

An ox may stomp on my plants.

An ox may stomp on me!

I will need to hide **myself** inside."

"It may be a frog.

Frogs are quite loud.

Frogs ribbit and ribbit and ribbit.

Dear me, I hope it's not a frog!"

Copyright © by Houghton Mifflin Harcourt Publishing Company. All rights reserved.

"Perhaps it will be clams.
Clams are not much fun.
I cannot invite clams for tea."

Just then, Hen and her **family** showed up.

Raccoon saw nothing wrong with hens.

"Nice to meet you!" shouted Raccoon.

"**Please** stop by for tea one day!"

 **Look Back and Respond**  **Read Together**

Check the answer.

1 **How does Raccoon feel at the beginning?**

☐ worried   ☐ excited

2 **Why doesn't Raccoon like frogs?**

☐ Frogs are loud.   ☐ Frogs are mean.

3 **Why doesn't Raccoon like clams?**

☐ Clams are not much fun.

☐ Clams make too much tea.

Write about Raccoon.

_____

4 **Raccoon is** _____.

Copyright © by Houghton Mifflin Harcourt Publishing Company. All rights reserved.

"The New Friend"
Student Book pp. 165–181

Be a Reading Detective!

Look back at "The New Friend."
Think about the questions.
Look for clues.

1 **Who** moves in next door?

2 **How** do the boys feel about their new neighbor?

Write or draw your answer.

1 **Who** moves in next door?

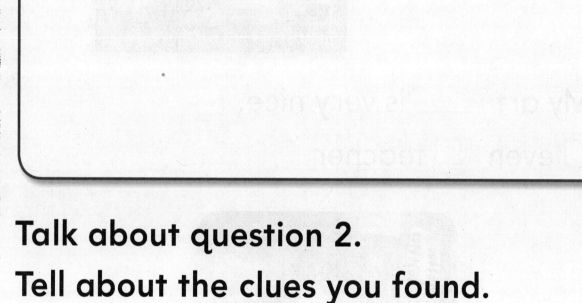

Talk about question 2.
Tell about the clues you found.

2 **How** do the boys feel about their new neighbor?

Copyright © by Houghton Mifflin Harcourt Publishing Company. All rights reserved.

even

studied

surprised

teacher

Art Class

Complete the sentence.

Check the best word.

1 My art _____ is very nice.

☐ even   ☐ teacher

2 I made it _____ better by adding blue.

☐ even   ☐ teacher

Copyright © by Houghton Mifflin Harcourt Publishing Company. All rights reserved.

3 Sol _____ each marker.

☐ surprised   ☐ studied

4 I _____ my mom with a gift!

☐ surprised   ☐ studied

Read the words in the word box.
Write the word under the picture.

napping	spotted
smiling	striped

1

2

3

4

Dog-Print Art

by Janice Winfield

It was raining.

Happy and I were not too happy.

We were bored, bored, bored.

Copyright © by Houghton Mifflin Harcourt Publishing Company. All rights reserved.

I got out paints and paper.

But then my pal Jenny **surprised** me.

"Ready Jill?" she asked.

"Let's go shopping!"

Shopping put me in a good mood.

But when we got back, that ended.

Footprints! Nose prints!

Dog prints on that nice clean paper!

Copyright © by Houghton Mifflin Harcourt Publishing Company. All rights reserved.

Happy's red nose gave him away.

At first I got really mad.

Then I **studied** Happy's art close up.

Copyright © by Houghton Mifflin Harcourt Publishing Company. All rights reserved.

I picked up Happy's painting.
I added dots and lines.
"It was not bad," I told Happy.
"But now it will be **even** better."

Mom thought so, too.

And Mom's an art **teacher**, so she knows!

After that, my good mood came back.

Not bad for a rainy day!

Check the answer.

1 How are Jill and Happy the same?

☐ They both paint.

☐ They are both always happy.

2 What does Jill do with Happy's art?

☐ throws it out ☐ makes it better

3 Jill's mood gets ____ by the end.

☐ better ☐ worse

Write about a rainy day.

_____

4 _____

_____

Copyright © by Houghton Mifflin Harcourt Publishing Company. All rights reserved.

Be a Reading Detective!

Look back at "The Dot."
Think about the questions.
Look for clues.

"The Dot"
Student Book pp. 15–33

Return to

1 What does Vashti learn?

2 How does Vashti's teacher help her?

Write or draw your answer.

1 What does Vashti learn?

Copyright © by Houghton Mifflin Harcourt Publishing Company. All rights reserved.

Talk about question 2.
Tell about the clues you found.

2 How does Vashti's teacher help her?

✓ WORDS TO KNOW

always

different

happy

stories

Our Talents

Complete the sentence.
Check the best word.

1 Sue tells the funniest _____.

☐ stories ☐ different

2 We are all good at _____ things.

☐ always ☐ different

3 Painting makes Britt _____.

☐ happy ☐ stories

4 Pam _____ wins at checkers.

☐ happy ☐ always

Copyright © by Houghton Mifflin Harcourt Publishing Company. All rights reserved.

Read the words in the word box.

Write the word under the picture.

> happy   happier
>
> messy   messier

1

_____

- - - - - - - - - - -

_____

2

_____

- - - - - - - - - - -

_____

3

_____

- - - - - - - - - - -

_____

4

_____

- - - - - - - - - - -

_____

What Can You Do?

by Megan Linke

Copyright © by Houghton Mifflin Harcourt Publishing Company. All rights reserved.

My pal Sammy tells jokes.

His **stories** are great.

Sam is the funniest kid!

He's much funnier than Kate.

Kate can't tell jokes.
She blows bubbles instead!
That Kate can blow bubbles
As big as her head.

Copyright © by Houghton Mifflin Harcourt Publishing Company. All rights reserved.

I wish mine got like that,
But that's not my thing.
What I am good at is singing.
I can sing like a king!

My pal Sally is smart.
She does math like a pro.
She can add and subtract
Ten times better than Jo.

But Jo is a pro
At her own kind of game.
She **always** makes goals.
She has really good aim!

Copyright © by Houghton Mifflin Harcourt Publishing Company. All rights reserved.

We each are quite **different**.

I am **happy** it's true!

Now, tell me, my friend,

Tell me, what can you do?

Look Back and Respond

Read Together

Check the answer.

1 **Why did the author write this?**

☐ to share a message

☐ to show how to do something

2 **What is page 115 about?**

☐ telling jokes

☐ playing soccer

3 **Why does the story rhyme?**

☐ so that it makes more sense

☐ so that it is more fun to read

Write about your own special skill.

4 _____

_ _ _ _ _ _ _ _ _ _ _ _ _ _ _ _ _ _ _ _

_____

Copyright © by Houghton Mifflin Harcourt Publishing Company. All rights reserved.

Return to

"What Can You Do?"
Student Book pp. 51–69

Be a Reading Detective!

Look back at "What Can You Do?"
Think about the questions.
Look for clues.

1 **What** can the children do?

2 **How** can you get better at something?

Write or draw your answer.

1 **What** can the children do?

Talk about question 2.

Tell about the clues you found.

2 **How** can you get better at something?

Copyright © by Houghton Mifflin Harcourt Publishing Company. All rights reserved.

cried

heard

large

should

I Can Do It!

Complete the sentence.
Check the best word.

1 We can lift this ____ box.

☐ large ☐ cried

2 "I win!" she ____.

☐ heard ☐ cried

3 Mom and Dad _____ me singing.

☐ heard   ☐ should

4 You _____ try out for the team!

☐ should   ☐ large

Copyright © by Houghton Mifflin Harcourt Publishing Company. All rights reserved.

Read the words in the word box.
Write the word under the picture.

light	pie
night	cry

1

_____

- - - - - - - - - - - - - - - -

_____

2

_____

- - - - - - - - - - - - - - - -

_____

3

_____

- - - - - - - - - - - - - - - -

_____

4

_____

- - - - - - - - - - - - - - - -

_____

Mighty Little Mole

by Paolo Rizzi

Copyright © by Houghton Mifflin Harcourt Publishing Company. All rights reserved.

One day, Mule came upon an odd thing. "Why, this looks like food!" said Mule. "How nice!"

Mule grabbed it and tugged.
But the **large** thing was stuck tight.

Copyright © by Houghton Mifflin Harcourt Publishing Company. All rights reserved.

"I cannot pick it up by myself," said Mule.

So Pig came up to help him.

"We **should** tie this rope on," said Pig.

Mole **heard** them crying.

"Can I help?" he asked.

"Don't be silly," grunted Mule.

"You are too little," gasped Pig.

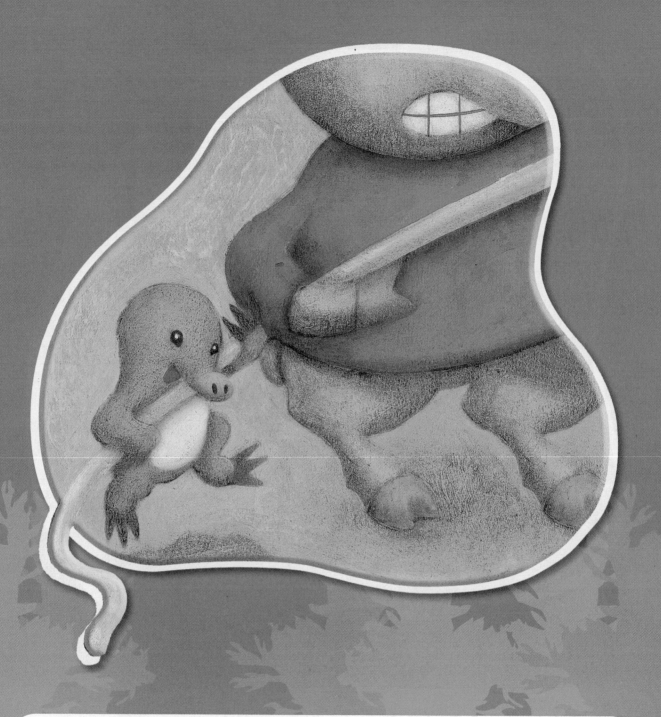

Copyright © by Houghton Mifflin Harcourt Publishing Company. All rights reserved.

But Mole had to try.
He grabbed the rope.
He tugged with all his might.

Pop! Little Mole had done it!

"Mighty Mole to the rescue!" yelled Mule.

"Dinner at my place!" **cried** Mole.

Look Back and Respond

Read Together

Check the answer.

1 Who are the characters in this story?

☐ Mule, Pig, and Mole

☐ a carrot and a piece of rope

2 Where does this story take place?

☐ at Mole's house ☐ outside

3 What is Mule's problem?

☐ He cannot get the carrot out.

☐ He has no friends.

Write about Mole.

4 Mole is _____ .

Copyright © by Houghton Mifflin Harcourt Publishing Company. All rights reserved.

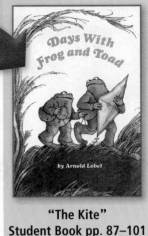

Return to

Days With Frog and Toad

by Arnold Lobel

"The Kite"
Student Book pp. 87–101

Be a Reading Detective!

Look back at "The Kite."
Think about the questions.
Look for clues.

① **What** do the robins say?

② **Why** does the kite fly in the end?

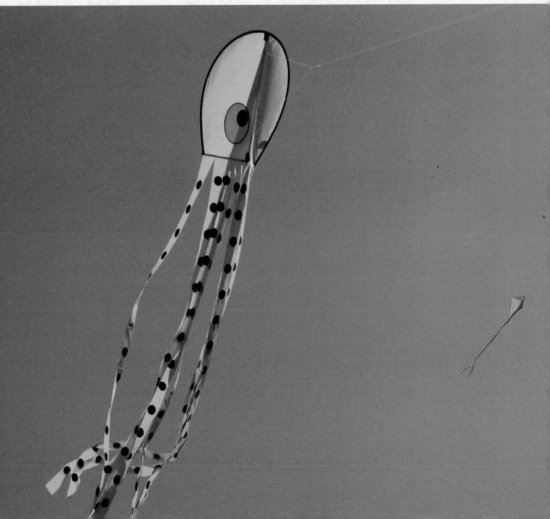

Write or draw your answer.

1 **What** do the robins say?

Talk about question 2.
Tell about the clues you found.

2 **Why** does the kite fly in the end?

Copyright © by Houghton Mifflin Harcourt Publishing Company. All rights reserved.

TiNY CRiTTeRS

caught

idea

minute

thought

Complete the sentence.

Check the best word.

① This animal _____ dinner in its web.

☐ caught ☐ idea

② Did you see the bug land?

In a _____, it will take off!

☐ thought ☐ minute

132

3 Before, I _____ all bugs were bad.

☐ thought ☐ idea

4 Now I know bugs can be helpful.
This is a new _____ for me!

☐ minute ☐ idea

Copyright © by Houghton Mifflin Harcourt Publishing Company. All rights reserved.

Read the words in the word box.
Write the word under the picture.

| helpful | sunny |
| playful | quickly |

1

2

3

4

Sick Day

by Paolo Rizzi

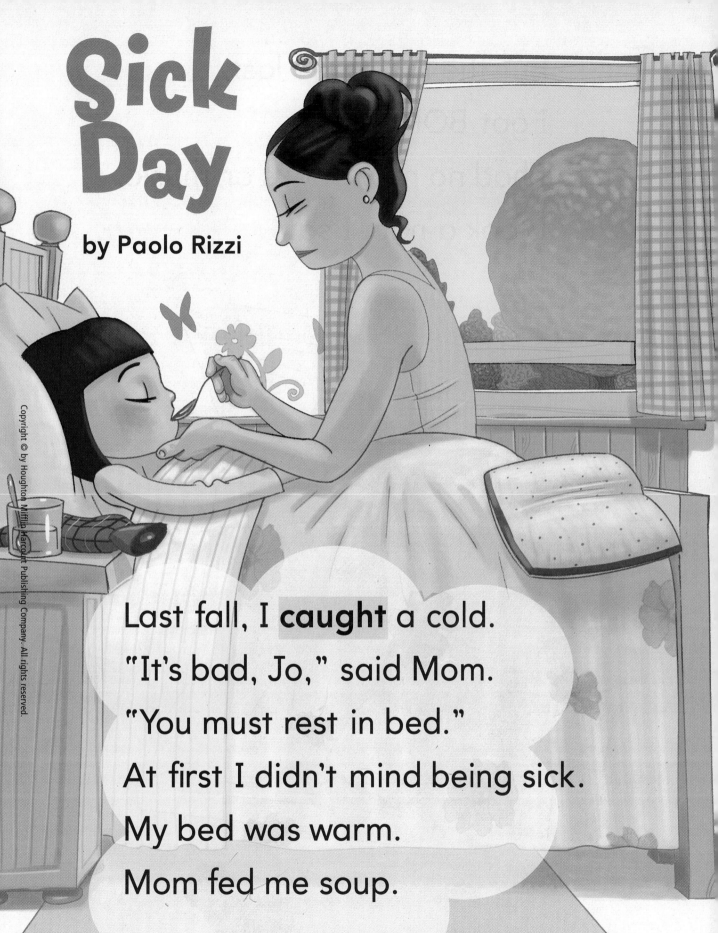

Copyright © by Houghton Mifflin Harcourt Publishing Company. All rights reserved.

Last fall, I **caught** a cold.

"It's bad, Jo," said Mom.

"You must rest in bed."

At first I didn't mind being sick.

My bed was warm.

Mom fed me soup.

But the fun didn't last.

I got BORED.

I had no new books or music.

I took a nap. I sat.

Copyright © by Houghton Mifflin Harcourt Publishing Company. All rights reserved.

As I sat, I saw a fly go by.

He flew slowly up.

Then he flew down.

The next **minute**, he made a

loop!

Then the fly landed near me.
I looked at his little legs.
He seemed to be waving.
I **thought** I was going mad!
But I said, "Hi, Fly."

Copyright © by Houghton Mifflin Harcourt Publishing Company. All rights reserved.

Then the fly did tricks for me.

He played fetch with a bead.

He flew in and out of hoops.

He was a champ!

I named him Bo.

I never saw Bo again.

My pals still laugh at the **idea**.

But I think Bo was my friend.

He did tricks to make me laugh.

I'm happy I met him.

Look Back and Respond

Check the answer.

1 **Why does Mom feed Jo soup?**

☐ because Jo is sick

☐ because Jo loves soup

2 **How does Jo feel at first?**

☐ She doesn't mind being sick.

☐ She is bored with being sick.

3 **How does Jo feel about Bo?**

☐ happy   ☐ angry

4 **Write about what Bo did.**

_____

- -

_____

Copyright © by Houghton Mifflin Harcourt Publishing Company. All rights reserved.

Return to

Tedd Arnold

"Hi! Fly Guy"
Student Book pp. 119–141

Be a Reading Detective!

Look back at "Hi! Fly Guy."
Think about the questions.
Look for clues.

1 **When** does Fly Guy meet Buzz?

2 **How** does Fly Guy help Buzz?

Write or draw your answer.

1 **When** does Fly Guy meet Buzz?

Talk about question 2.
Tell about the clues you found.

2 **How** does Fly Guy help Buzz?

Copyright © by Houghton Mifflin Harcourt Publishing Company. All rights reserved.

everyone

field

loved

most

Kick It!

Complete the sentence.

Check the best word.

1. The players ran up the _____.

   ☐ everyone ☐ field

2. Our team plays _____ days.

   ☐ most ☐ loved

3 When she scored, _____ cheered.

☐ everyone ☐ field

4 They _____ being part of a team.

☐ loved ☐ most

Copyright © by Houghton Mifflin Harcourt Publishing Company. All rights reserved.

Read the words in the word box.
Write the word under the picture.

music	open
baby	donut

1

_____

- - - - - - - - - - - -

_____

2

_____

- - - - - - - - - - - -

_____

3

_____

- - - - - - - - - - - -

_____

4

_____

- - - - - - - - - - - -

_____

Soccer Sisters

by Roberto Gómez

Copyright © by Houghton Mifflin Harcourt Publishing Company. All rights reserved.

Edith and Meg both **loved** soccer.

Most times, this was a good thing.

But not always.

One day, Mom was driving them home.

Meg's team had just played.

"You played so well, Meg!" said Edith.

"I hope I can play like that on Friday!"

Copyright © by Houghton Mifflin Harcourt Publishing Company. All rights reserved.

Meg stopped smiling.

"You are playing on Friday?" she asked.

"I am too! You'll be playing my team!"

After that, the sisters were not pals.

"I can run faster than you!" growled Edith.

"I can kick harder than you!" growled Meg.

Copyright © by Houghton Mifflin Harcourt Publishing Company. All rights reserved.

On the big day, Edith ran up the **field**.

Pow! When she scored, **everyone** cheered.

Meg cheered as well.

She even forgot that she was mad.

"You know," said Meg,
"it does not matter who wins.
Playing with you is so much fun."
"I think so, too," said Edith. "Let's play!"

 **Look Back and Respond**  **Read Together**

Check the answer.

1 **What is the story mostly about?**

☐ two sisters   ☐ two cousins

2 **Why did Edith and Meg get upset?**

☐ They had to stop playing soccer.

☐ They had to play against each other.

3 **What lesson do the girls learn?**

☐ Playing together is no fun.

☐ It does not matter who wins.

Write about your favorite sport.

4 _____

- - - - - - - - - - - - - - - - - - -

_____

Copyright © by Houghton Mifflin Harcourt Publishing Company. All rights reserved.

Be a Reading Detective!

Return to

"Winners Never Quit!"
Student Book pp. 159–177

Look back at "Winners Never Quit!"

Think about the questions.

Look for clues.

1 **Why** does Mia quit?

2 **What** does Mia learn?

Write or draw your answer.

1 **Why** does Mia quit?

Talk about question 2.
Tell about the clues you found.

2 **What** does Mia learn?

Copyright © by Houghton Mifflin Harcourt Publishing Company. All rights reserved.

Summarize Strategy

You can **summarize** what you read.

- Tell important ideas in your own words.

- Tell ideas in an order that makes sense.

- Keep the meaning of the text.

- Use only a few sentences.

Analyze/Evaluate Strategy

You can **analyze** and **evaluate** a text. Think carefully about what you read. Form an opinion about it.

1. Think about the text and the author.
   - What are the important facts and ideas?
   - What does the author want you to know?

2. Decide what is important. Then form an opinion.
   - How do you feel about what you read?
   - Do you agree with the author's ideas?

Copyright © by Houghton Mifflin Harcourt Publishing Company. All rights reserved.

Infer/Predict Strategy

Use clues to figure out what the author does not tell you. Then you are making an **inference**.

Use clues to figure out what will happen next. Then you are making a **prediction**.

Monitor/Clarify Strategy

Monitor what you read. Make sure it makes sense.

Find a way to understand what does not.

- Reread.
- Read ahead.
- Ask questions.

Question Strategy

Ask yourself **questions** as you read.

Look for answers.

Some questions to ask:

- What does the author mean?

- Who or what is this about?

- Why did this happen?

- What is the main idea?

Visualize Strategy

You can **visualize**.

- Make pictures in your mind as you read.

- Use words in the text to help you.

- Make pictures of people, places, things, and actions.

Copyright © by Houghton Mifflin Harcourt Publishing Company. All rights reserved.

PHOTO CREDITS

Placement Key: (r) right, (l) left, (c) center, (t) top, (b) bottom, (bg) background

2 (t) © Image Ideas. 3 (t) © PhotoDisc, Inc. 3 (b) © Corbis. 4 (tl) © Comstock. 4 (tr) © Comstock. 4 (bl) © Getty Images/PhotoDisc. 4 (br) © PhotoDisc, Inc. 11A Comstock/Jupiterimages/Getty Images. 11B NASA photo, courtesy of the Lunar and Planetary Institute. 12 (b) © PhotoDisc, Inc. 13 (c) © Getty Images/PhotoDisc. 14 (tl) © PhotoDisc, Inc. 14 (tr) © PhotoDisc, Inc. 14 (bl) © Rubberball Productions. 14 (br) © PhotoDisc, Inc. 21A © Image Source Pink/Alamy. 22 (t) © Corbis. 24 (tr) © Artville. 24 (bl) © Comstock, Inc. 24 (tl) © PhotoDisc/Getty Images. 24 (br) © Getty Images/PhotoDisc. 25–30 (ant) © Photospin. 31A © Comstock Images/Getty Images. 31A (c) © Getty Images. 31A (c) © Comstock/Getty Images. 31B © Digital Vision/Getty Images. 31B © Getty Images. 32 (b) © Corbis. 34 (tl) © Comstock. 34 (bl) © Brand X/Punchstock. 34 (tr) © Getty Images/PhotoDisc. 34 (br) © PhotoDisc, Inc. 36 (br) © PhotoDisc, Inc. 36 (t) © Photospin. 37 © Artville. 38 © Comstock. 41A Digital Vision/Getty Images. 41B © Houghton Mifflin Harcourt. 42 (b) © Corel Stock Photo Library. 42 (t) © Getty Images/PhotoDisc. 43 (t) © Corel Stock Photo Library. 43 (b) © Larry Bones/Getty Images. 44 (tl) © PhotoDisc, Inc. 44 (tr) © EyeWire. 44 (bl) © Image Club. 44 (br) © PhotoDisc, Inc. 51A © Fotolia. 51B © Digital Vision/Getty Images. 52 Getty Images/PhotoDisc. 52 © Wong Hock Weng/Alamy Images. 53 ©Jupiterimages/Getty Images. 55 DAJ/Getty Images. 55 © Getty Images. 57 © Getty Images. 57 Digital Vision/Getty Images. 58 © PhotoDisc/Getty Images. 59 © PhotoDisc/Getty Images. 59 Brand X Pictures/Jupiterimages/Getty Images. 60 © DAJ/Getty Images. 61 © PhotoDisc/Getty Images. 61A (b) Comstock/Getty Images. 61B (bl, bc, br) Comstock/Getty Images. 62 (c) © Digital Stock, Corbis Corporation. 62 (b) © Photolink. 62 (t) © Artville/Getty Images. 63 (t) © Getty Images/Digital Vision. 63 (b) © Stockbyte/Getty Images. 64 (tl) © Getty Images/PhotoDisc. 64 (tr) © PhotoDisc, Inc. 64 (bl) © Getty Images/PhotoDisc. 64 (br) © Getty Images/PhotoDisc. 71A (b) © Cristina Lichti/Flickr/Photolibrary. 71B (b) © Houghton Mifflin Harcourt. 72 (b) © Getty Images/Brand X Pictures. 73 (t) © PhotoDisc. 73 (c) © Stockbyte/Getty Images. 74 (tl) © Artville. 74 (tr) © Corbis. 74 (bl) © Getty Images/Stockdisk. 74 (br) © Corbis. 75 (tl & bl) © Stockdisk/Getty Images. 75 (tc) © Getty Images/Rubberball Productions. 75 (tr) © Getty Images Royalty Free. 75 (bc) © Getty Images Royalty Free. 75 (br) © PhotoDisc, Inc. 76 (b) © Stockdisk/Getty Images. 78 (b) © Getty Images Royalty Free. 79 (r) © PhotoDisc, Inc. 80 (l) © Getty Images Royalty Free. 80 (c) © Stockdisk/Getty Images. 80 (r) © Getty Images/Rubberball Productions. 81 © Stockdisk/Getty Images. 81A (b) © PhotoDisc/Getty Images. 81B (b) © Digital Vision/Getty Images. 81B (b) Comstock/Getty Images. 82 Comstock/Getty Images. 83 © Comstock/Getty Images. 83 Luedke and Sparrow/Getty Images. 85 © Artville/Getty Images. 85 Image Source/Corbis. 85 Photodisc/Getty Images. 86 Luedke and Sparrow/Getty Images. 86 Photodisc/Getty Images. 87 © Doug Menuez/Photodisc/Getty Images. 87 Photodisc Green (Royalty-free)/Getty Images. 87 © Getty Images. 88 © HMH. 89 © Comstock/Getty Images. 89 Photodisc/Getty Images. 89 Brand X Pictures/Getty Images. 90 Getty Images. 91 © Artville/Getty Images. 91 Brand X Pictures/Getty Images. 91A (b) © Houghton Mifflin Harcourt. 91B (b) Creatas/Jupiterimages/Getty Images. 92 (b) © Getty Images/PhotoDisc. 93 (t) © PictureQuest. 94 (tl) © PhotoDisc, Inc. 94 (tr) © Comstock. 94 (bl) © PhotoDisc, Inc. 94 (br) © PhotoDisc, Inc. 101A (b) © Houghton Mifflin Harcourt. 101B (b) © Judith Collins/Alamy Images. 101B (b) Brand X Pictures/Getty Images. 102 (b) © Corbis. 104 (tl) © PhotoDisc, Inc. 104 (tr) © Comstock. 104 (br) © Getty Images/Digital Vision. 104 (bl) © PhotoDisc, Inc. 111A (b) Creatas/Jupiterimages/Getty Images. 111B (b) Comstock/Getty Images. 112 (b) © Getty Images/Blend. 114 (tr) © Getty Images/Digital Vision. 114 (tl) © Getty Images/Digital Vision. 115 (bg) © PhotoDisc, Inc. 115 (tl) © PhotoDisc, Inc. 115 (tr) © PhotoDisc, Inc. 115 (b) © Getty Images Royalty Free. 116 (bg) © Corbis. 117 (bg) © PhotoDisc, Inc. 117 (t) © PhotoDisc, Inc. 117 (br) © Getty Images/PhotoDisc. 118 © Getty Images/PhotoDisc. 119 © Getty Images/PhotoDisc. 120 © PhotoDisc/Getty Images. 121 © PhotoDisc, Inc. 121A (b) Creatas/Jupiterimages/Getty Images. 121B (b) © Comstock/Getty Images. 121B (b) © Houghton Mifflin Harcourt. 122 (b) © Image 100/Corbis. 123 (t) © PhotoDisc/Getty Images. 123 (b) © Corbis. 124 (tl) © Corbis. 124 (bl) © Getty Images/PhotoDisc. 124 (tr) © EyeWire/Getty Images. 124 (br) © Corbis. 131A (b) © Houghton Mifflin Harcourt. 131B (b) Creatas/Jupiterimages/Getty Images. 131B (b) HMH. 132 © Getty Images. 133 © Radius Images/Getty Images. 141A (b) © Houghton Mifflin Harcourt. 141A (b) © RTimages/Alamy. 141B (b) © opus/a.collectionRF/Getty Images. 142 (t) © Corbis. 142 (b) © Shutterstock. 143 (t) © Corel Stock Photo Library. 144 (tr) © Getty Images/PhotoDisc. 144 (bl) © Stockbyte/Getty Images. 144 (tl) © Getty Images/PhotoDisc. 151A (b) Photodisc/Getty Images. 151B (b) Creatas/Jupiterimages/Getty Images. 151B (b) © Comstock/Getty Images. All other images property of HMH Publishers.